CONSEQUENCES TO
SUCCESS

CONSEQUENCES TO SUCCESS

Life lessons—drawing from valuable skills and personal experiences, encouraging character development and gratitude, and showing what YOU are capable of achieving.

Sophia Johnson

authorHOUSE®

AuthorHouse™
1663 Liberty Drive
Bloomington, IN 47403
www.authorhouse.com
Phone: 1-800-839-8640

Published by AuthorHouse   10/25/2012

ISBN: 978-1-4772-3919-3 (sc)
ISBN: 978-1-4772-3920-9 (e)

Acknowledgments

Thank you to God who has given me the strength each day to succeed and believe in myself, enabling me to write this book.

Much love to my babies Laurelle, Laakan, Amani and Ashia; mummy's four blessings. I am so proud of you all; you are the reason why I continue. You all will achieve your goals, because you are great and you have the ability. Thanks to Laakan, my gifted, talented son, who named this book.

Thank you to the authors who I have mentioned in the further reading section, as your books resonated with me, as much now as ever. Special thanks to Mr Tyrese Gibson, yes sir, your book and daily tweets held meaning for me, and you have been stellar on days when I needed a boost.

Thank you to my great friend Annette Archer, always there at the right time. God bless you.

Thank you to pastor Trevor Smith for delivering the Word with so much impact each Sunday.

Thank you to my cousin, friend, brother and confidant Daniel Thorpe. You have been, and still are, there, every step of the way. God bless your career and goals.

Thank you to my cousin and business partner Dionne for always supporting me, and always being there to help with the children. I love you.

Thank you to my grandfather, who has been the best man in my life, always by my side. Love you, Dad.

Thank you to the readers for sharing my story. I hope and pray and have faith that something in this book touches you and makes a positive difference in your life; all I have done is shared my story and been real with you, in order to give you strength and motivation, as your experiences are also **consequences to success.**

Wishing You ALL the best,

Sophia

CONTENTS

"All great achievements require time" ~ Maya Angelou

FOREWORD

I had an epiphany one day. I realised that, successful though I was, I wasn't giving myself the recognition or the gratitude I deserved for my successes. People often define success in materialistic terms: cars, houses, jewellery. But is that really success? How do we measure our true success? This book aims to enable you to embrace your life experiences, and to see that your growth as a person is a major success in itself.

How will I spread my message to others? This was the main question I asked myself. Why do I feel the need to write this book? Well, it's because I have a story to tell, and the more I read other authors' books, the more I realise that my personal growth should be shared with others, and that my help and support should be offered to people as they undergo their own journeys in life. I have recently taken on projects which give back to the community; and as a mother, businesswoman, coach, philanthropist, author and, hopefully, an agent of change, I aim to give back what lessons I have learned, in order to assist others. In truth this has been hard; however, with knowledge, and a certain consistent light from within, comes the faith to persist.

I have a family to take care of, with four blessings—my children. Yet I am also still finding myself; my growth is continuous, and I know that actually I have to develop and change. I love what I do, I love sharing what I have learned, helping individuals to find their true purpose and make changes in their lives which they are proud of. This book of memoirs, with its detailed messages and action words, is for the reader to engage with, and hopefully will bring about a better, more confident you.

Each day I wake up with a burning sensation within, an urgent awareness that I have to achieve certain goals to take me to the greater place that I know is just around the corner. In every experience there is something for us all to learn and act upon; some may see this as the 'law of attraction,' others may believe in signs from a higher being, from God, as I do. All I really ask, though, is for you to read this book and take something from it; use the experiences documented within it positively, as **consequences to success.**

"It's better to conquer yourself than to win a thousand battles"
~ Kimora Lee Simmons
"Therefore I tell you, whatever you ask for in prayer, believe
that you received it, and it will be yours" ~ Mark 11: 24, New
International Version of the Bible
"Our path is the way we travel, our vision is where we travel,
our purpose is why we travel" ~Kevin Hall
"You can be rich in the pocket and poor in the mind"
~ Sophia Johnson

CHAPTER ONE

Building your foundation

I was born in 1975. My mother was young, and still living
with her parents and three siblings, when she had me. My
father was also young, and had been in the country for five
years living with his aunt, as he was born in the Caribbean.
Happiness abounded in my family when I was born, as a
baby hadn't graced the home with its presence for 12 years;
but a kind of disappointment was also there, as my mother
had fallen pregnant just as she had left school. Growing
up, I was the centre of attention within the home, and my
grandmother took me as her own. Old-school Caribbean
nurturing was the order of the day; full of food, discipline,
jokes and so much love. My biological parents were like my
aunt and uncle, and that sat well with them; they came and
went as they pleased, acting like friends with the common
bond of a child. When I was two, my mother said that she
was moving out. This was fine with my grandparents; she
was 19, had completed her nursing course, and now wanted
to be more independent. On the day of packing, she was told

that she couldn't take me with her, just starting out on her newfound life as she was. Therefore the decision was made to leave me with my grandparents, and then, when my mother was settled, she could come and get me. Now, many may think that this was too overpowering a stance on the part my grandparents, but my grandmother, in her wisdom, knew that my mother needed to learn to cope for herself and grow, and, also, I feel that it was my grandmother's opportunity to teach me understanding, awareness and key skills. Childhood time with my real parents was rare, with visits mostly confined to birthdays and Christmas. I learned, though, that 'what you don't know doesn't hurt you,' and besides, the love and affection of my grandparents made up for it tenfold. My grandmother was a seamstress and a cook, so each day she would be at the machine, multi-tasking, baking Caribbean dishes made to order for friends and acquaintances. She was a mother of four and her daily life followed a set routine. Without fail, dinner was on the table at 6pm, just in time for when my grandfather came home from work. He also adhered to his daily, uniformed routine, returning home from work at 5pm, washing, and presenting himself at the table ready for his meal. My grandfather, a self-employed carpenter, always worked hard, was reputable, and thrived in his field. I remember being about eight years old and him coming home and saying (in his deep Jamaican accent): "Sophia, I am doing work in that woman's house on TV, I can't remember her name." Then, for about an hour, each name I blurted out met the same reply: "No, no, no," and then "I will remember soon, stop bothering me." Two weeks later, he announced that her name was Annie Lennox. "Oh wow," I thought, "Dad (as I called him), take me with you so I can meet her, please?" But he said he'd finished the job already. I felt crushed at this; I'm not saying he did it on purpose, but what a lost opportunity, I thought. Through the years this became one of those stories my family enjoyed telling.

I lived in the family home with my grandparents, three other children, my aunty and two uncles. My aunt was quiet and obedient to her parents, working nine to five in an office. My elder uncle was hard-working yet blessed with a loving heart. He was always misunderstood as ignorant; but really he just was strong-minded and needed to be supported in his views. From a young age he decided to become a vegetarian, which was almost unheard of in our Caribbean home where the weekly menu consisted of pigtail, oxtail and butterbeans. My Nan always offered him bacon for breakfast on Sunday, just to see if he was sure. He later started to twist his hair and follow the Rastafarian movement. And yes, he is still a Rasta. My younger uncle, a hands-on worker, always saw himself as the joker of the household. In the end, I learned to love my family no matter what. If I liken my childhood life to that of a worker, it's because I was always learning a skill: reading the newspaper to my Nan from around five years old, learning to cook the many dishes that she cooked daily, closely watching as she stitched garments. She was partially sighted, so it was my duty to read to her and support her, and I loved it. After a few years Nan started to suffer from ill health, including blood pressure and blackouts, which hospitalised her on a few occasions. This led me to cook more in the home. By the time I was nine years old my aunt had moved out, but would come to the house in the daytime while I was at school, to tidy and make food for Nan. I would come home from school and feed her, joke with her, and then maybe play outside with friends for an hour, but always making sure to have a meal on the table for granddad at 6pm. It was all a routine which I followed, even when Nan became forgetful and unwell and ended up in hospital. One night I was curled up beside Nan in bed, just the way it had always been for the ten years of my life, and I remember being woken up by my aunt. 'What's she doing here in the middle of the night?' I wondered. I was put in my room, which I didn't sleep in often. 'Oh my,' I thought. My aunt told me they were going to hospital with Nan. Ok, I thought, it's another episode of illness, another routine to follow. I went straight back to sleep. In the morning a brown suitcase was at the foot of the stairs. Granddad was making me hot chocolate. 'What's come over him?' I asked myself, as it was odd to find him in the kitchen. He told me to sit down and drink. As I did, he said "we took Birdie to hospital last night." 'Yeah I know that,' I thought, remembering the suitcase at the stairs. But then granddad broke the news to me that Nan had died. I started to shake instantly, my hot chocolate spilling on my hands and lap. I was silent; my world had changed forever. Yet I heard her voice say 'don't cry, I will always be with you,' as though she was there with me. The following days went quickly by, as the house filled with people I didn't regularly see and with vast portions of food. Those around me cried in grief, yet I never did. Why didn't I cry? Because Nan was still with me. I felt her, and I could even smell her. Her lingering presence comforted me. On the ninth day a family meeting was convened, with the women in the family, my granddad, neighbours who had been friends for years, my granddad's two sisters, and my aunt. They decided, since leaving me to live in the house with granddad and two uncles wasn't the best option, that I would live with my aunt.

I had grown up with my aunt, so it wasn't as if I was moving in with strangers. She now had two children, a boy and a girl. I loved the little boy and was very close to him; when my aunt had visited my Nan each day to tend to her she used to bring him along, and I would sit with him for hours. My cousins were two years apart, and there was always something to do or help with. I moved in with them just as I was finishing primary school; this was a little difficult to cope with, as living in a different area meant parting ways with friends I had been with from nursery. I did have one close friend though, two years my senior, who went to the same primary school as me, and who I would still see. Her grandmother lived opposite my grandmother and they were best friends, always together. Since I called my biological grandmother Nan, I called my friend's Nan grandma. I knew this friend from the day I was born, and even after I had moved, I frequently slept at her house at weekends. It felt like home. At my actual home, meanwhile, I could now have my own room, and I acquired a sense of independence early on, which became embedded in me. If ever I needed independence, I needed it now! My aunt made sure there was food in the house; my grandfather visited and helped support her; my parents continued to come by on occasion. Yet I missed the singing, the hugs and kisses, the heartfelt talking, the jokes that the heartfelt talking led to. What a great mother and lady my Nan was, and what a great amount I had learned and was capable of at such a tender age! Things had changed for me, not by my choice, but through life's challenges. These moments happen to everyone. I didn't know then that my first ten years were what made me, and what would keep me going.

Message:

We all may have read books, watched films, or indeed made our own studies about the early stages of growing up. We can certainly agree that these tender years are highly formative. If you reflect on the surroundings in

which you were brought up, you can use this to make a list of your key positive personality traits. For example, as a child I showed strength and adaptability, in bouncing back and not giving up on my life despite many things which might have upset me greatly had I let them. These sorts of character attributes are the foundations, the things that will keep you going through thick and thin. "If we do not plant knowledge when young, it will give us no shade when we are old." ~ Lord Chesterfield

The action word is:

Courage. The ability to face danger, difficulty, uncertainty, or pain without being overcome by fear or being deflected from a chosen course of action. Start by implementing our action word, that is, being courageous, for a week—be bold in the decisions you make, stick to them, and deal with things head on. Try not to be negative, but rather to ask yourself: what am I learning at this moment? Is it really beyond me to cope? Courageously tackle the situation you find yourself in, even if it involves a seemingly trivial task such as phoning the utility company about a bill, and you may discover that no, coping is NOT beyond you! You will also find that usually, things do not turn out as badly as you fear they will. Once past the first obstacle, your strength and understanding will feed on itself and grow, giving you the confidence of your courage. The week of courageous action can then become a month . . . or longer.

"Your life does not get better by chance, it gets better by change" ~ John Rohn
"(C)hoices (H)appiness (A)mbition (N)urturing (G)reatness (E)xciting" ~ Sophia Johnson

CHAPTER TWO

All experiences are signs

I was a clever child, but continued with school more out of necessity than anything else. I was not making the effort that I needed to make. No adult ever asked me how I was doing at school, or what I wanted to be. People, places, everything around me; all seemed like a struggle. I was well known at school for my mouth: feisty, funny, I always had an answer. I loved everyone and always wanted to help, yet early on I realised that, with some individuals, you can give but you won't receive. I longed for someone to really love me. I passed my exams; I had to, so that I wouldn't get myself unclassified like the majority of my peers. Many of my friends had children when they left school. I had a boyfriend but I wanted more. I went to college to study health and social care, which I found boring, but it would allow me to get a certificate and to work. Life at home was hard. I was reminded often that I should be grateful to have lived with my aunt in a house. I was already a breadwinner by this point, bringing in money, and by the age of 15 I was told I had to cook my own meals. This was fine with me; I was an excellent cook and was fed up with 'rustled up' food anyhow. I *was* truly grateful that my aunt had taken me under her wing, but when she went on holiday with her friends and her two kids, I had to stay at my mum's and that felt weird for me. I had a sister, four years younger. But within a week I knew I couldn't stay. My mum loved to drink alcohol, and this often turned a well-meaning plan for a lovely meal into a burnt pot and jam sandwiches all round. I had met my first boyfriend when I was 14, and at 19 we were still together. I fell pregnant at this age and we were happy. He had many issues of his own: his parents argued, his father was a drinker too, and having to fend for himself led him to hustling on the street. He had a good heart though, and we could talk for hours. We had each other's backs, too. Unfortunately, in his desperation to earn money he started smoking drugs; I knew instantly, but all I could ask was that he not do it in my presence. At seven months pregnant, I went for a check-up, and was told that the baby was small for its age. I was immediately put on a monitor, and phoned my aunt within hours. Then I was told I had to stay in the hospital, as the blood flow to the baby was too low. By the evening, my aunt and boyfriend were at my bedside, and the doctor said that I was to be moved the next day to another hospital, where a Caesarean could be performed. I barely slept a wink. I rubbed my stomach, hoping to feel the baby kicking, but by 4am all was still quiet. I was getting anxious, but maybe I was just worrying about nothing. Morning came, and my transfer was looming, but still I felt no kicking. The nurse called another nurse, who called a doctor. I was just 19 years old, and the one thing I thought I had full control of was slipping away from me. I went into labour, which was not even painful; notwithstanding the effect of the drugs I'd been given, I was emotionally numb. My boyfriend was in tears, and I just watched him. On 6 October 1994, I gave birth to a beautiful baby girl. I lay there wishing she would move, or open her eyes; I wished I could breathe life into her. My boyfriend cradled her and cried. Hours went by. Then, I smelt a familiar smell. I turned to my aunt and said everything is ok, Nanny is here, she has come for the baby. My aunt broke down, perhaps thinking I was on the verge of a breakdown of my own. But Nan *was* there, I could smell her.

I had to jump straight back into things. I was quite ill; my body had been through a great shock, rendering me bedridden for a few weeks. My boyfriend turned to the streets again. One day, though, I vowed to myself, as I lay in bed, that I was going to be the greatest I could be; that I hadn't been through such trauma for nothing. I decided to discuss with my aunt the possibility of going back to college and on to university, because I wanted to pursue a career in media. She said ok, but that she wanted me to look for somewhere to live for me and my boyfriend, and she'd give me half the deposit. Wow, I was stunned; she was basically telling me to forget my dreams, and just get my head down and work and pay bills instead. But I took her words on the chin, knowing that maybe I wasn't in the soundest state of mind emotionally, and started to look for new accommodation. A few short weeks later, I found a flat in the middle of the ghetto, and also secured a job as a marketing executive for a computer company. My boyfriend started working in the factory, assembling the computers. Time passed, and I worked, paid the bills and got on with it all. It was just me and my boyfriend. I visited my family weekly, but it seemed like their job was done; that they had cared for me until I was old enough, and then they had let me go. After a year in our one-bedroom flat, I felt that it was all somewhat frightening, without my family. I conceived again a few months after my stillborn child. This pregnancy wasn't planned, but we both were happy, not to mention nervous, considering what we had been through. I was truly taken care of by the hospital, with regular checks and medication to make sure the new baby and I were healthy. My boyfriend was involved as a defendant in a court case involving a robbing, but we weren't really anxious, as we knew it was wrongful identity. We visited the solicitor as a formality. After our first court appearance we had planned to go shopping; when we arrived at court we were told the case had been adjourned and was going to take place in the Crown Court. We didn't know exactly how or why this was happening. The victim of the robbing knew by boyfriend as their factory was opposite his best friend's house; he saw them meet their daily. The day in court came. On the last day of trial, as the verdict was due, a funny feeling appeared in my stomach. Was it a gut feeling, or my baby's first flutter? (I was now 16 weeks pregnant, and we hadn't told anyone yet). The verdict was four years imprisonment . . . I couldn't believe it! The solicitor turned to me in a flash and said we'd appeal, as there wasn't enough evidence. Of course there wasn't enough evidence, I thought; my boyfriend isn't the one who did it. Our new baby was to be born without her dad being there; I was shocked. My pregnancy was proceeding well though, and I kept myself busy learning how to drive, working, and visiting the prison every fortnight. The prison chaplain asked me to tell our story. When he had heard what had happened, he tried to persuade my boyfriend to tell the media that a grave injustice had been committed. Neither he nor I could convince him though. The chaplain kindly allowed us weekly visits in a separate room (his office, in fact). Labour Day came. Our beautiful daughter was born at 9.30pm.My boyfriend was permitted to be on the phone for the hour leading up to her birth, and he heard her first cry. I stayed with my aunt for the first eight weeks of my daughter's life, but intended to move into our new flat before being asked to leave. I decorated the new flat while at my aunt's, to make a better home for me and my baby. I continued visiting my boyfriend and awaited his release. When my daughter was one year old I registered her at a private nursery, and began work at a sales company. My daughter was my pride and joy; I would play and joke with her, cook great meals with her, hug her often, and constantly tell her that I loved her and that she was the best girl in the world. I tried to comfort my incarcerated boyfriend, but his attitude was that even the innocent end up in jail. Our daughter was two and a half when he was finally freed; and now he had to try to keep his head above water.

Message: reflective time

Within my short memoir, a lot of significant things occurred. Life can be like a rollercoaster ride. Often we seek advice from people who have not been through the same experience. Kevin Hall, in his book 'Aspire,' has a great quote: 'You cannot teach what you don't know and you cannot grow where you don't sow.' When you're being battered by a storm, be patient, be quiet, observe, and only speak when you are called to do so, when dialogue will move you forward. Often the wisest path to take is that of waiting, of understanding that the present situation will pass and is not forever; and that those experiences which hurt the most now are actually the best catalysts to advance you to the next level of your life.

The action word is:

Change. Look at situations in your life: were they self-created, or brought about by circumstances? You need to embrace change in every way. Before a decision, think 'how does this make me feel?' 'What am I going to achieve?' Or, as a great coach once told me, 'How does this situation serve me?' Do the exact opposite of what you may normally do; change the way you look, act, react to things; change the way you plan the future, even if this just amounts to altering the day you tend to set aside for household chores, for example. Embody change as part of your persona; and try to get rid of negativity while you're at it. Give it a go!

"There are two primary choices in life: to accept conditions as they exist, or accept the responsibility for changing them." ~ Denis Waitley

"When things look like they are against you, focus more, work harder, meditate on your visions . . . push through; the next experience, the next level, is fast approaching." ~ Sophia Johnson

CHAPTER THREE

What you're thinking is what you're attracting

At 24, I met someone who my peers from senior school knew, and apparently he always had a crush on me. I had a casual boyfriend at the time, but nothing serious, so I thought let's see. Whirlwind romance it may have been, but the new man loved me, and waited on me hand and foot; and he loved my daughter too. I had started work for the government, in a solid position that allowed me to take care of my needs. All I was looking for now was someone to love. My new boyfriend, six months into our relationship, had arranged for my aunt to look after my daughter and had booked us into a fine hotel. As we lay on the bed, he asked me to pass the remote under the pillow. A gorgeous engagement ring was there. He asked me to marry him, and I didn't even think about saying no. After one year together we were married.

On our honeymoon, though, he gave me cause to start doubting our relationship. 'Oh my god! What have I done?' I thought, and sadly things went downhill from there. People may say that there were no signs that something was wrong; but the signs were in fact there, when he was with his (so-called) friends and family. I was just too besotted by his apparent affection towards me and my beloved baby girl to notice the warnings. But now, knowing that what I was subjecting myself to I was also subjecting my daughter to, I had to get out. I had to stop blaming myself for other people's behaviour, too. I was losing so much weight from stress that I didn't even hide it from my family. I was crying out for help and they didn't answer. I fell pregnant again a year later, but was too weak and drained to even consider an abortion. I had lost a child once before, and knew how painful it was, so I was determined to have this baby. Six months into the pregnancy I had to go to hospital; my waters had broken. I gave birth to a son, who weighed two pounds and three ounces. My aunt, mum and husband all left after the birth, they didn't even go to the special care unit to see my baby. Wired up with drips and everything else, I begged the nurse to take me down in a wheelchair to see and smell and touch my son. As I sat there, I prayed: 'Lord have mercy upon my soul, give this child great health, help him to grow, let angels surround him . . . and dear Lord please help me, I can no longer live in this situation and subject my children to such fear . . . in Jesus' name I pray. Amen.' My son stayed in the hospital for three months and three blood transfusions, pulling through strong, healthy and handsome in the end. I was so proud. My daughter cuddled him daily and showed so much love and care for her baby brother. I felt that I had to strive to give them every opportunity and happiness in life.

Two days after our son returned from hospital, his father had a motorbike accident; I received a call saying he was in hospital. Upon my arrival there were so many people, it was as though the whole neighbourhood had arrived. He had fallen from his bike and snapped his spinal cord. The doctor took his mum and me into a room, and said that the outlook wasn't good; and that if he showed no signs of movement within 48 hours he'd be paralysed from the waist down. I couldn't cry, I was in so much shock. He didn't show the signs of movement, and became paralysed as we feared he might. His mind, though, was all over the place; each day when I visited the hospital and bathed him, he would curse and throw things. It was a massive transformation in his character. The time came for his release, and I suggested he stay at his mother's home. This proved a highly unpopular decision: his depression turned into actual dislike of me, and of everything else, and for the next year I was subjected to obscene phone calls, death threats, and disturbances at my home. This made each day a horrific experience, as one can imagine. I decided to move out of my home for a year; I had my children to think of. I found a solicitor, and filed for divorce.

Message:

People, in their suffering, regularly say" I cannot shake this feeling," or "I'm stuck in a rut." I maintain that saying these words, thinking these negative thoughts, actually attracts more torment, creates more of the very turmoil we seek to avoid. Thoughts have this power. Your gut feelings, your conscience, are there to enable you to consider and evaluate situations, so act upon these feelings of hope; embrace them and trust them, asking yourself "how can I move forward positively?" Think positive thoughts, so as to attract positive things. "The law of attraction is always working, whether you believe it or understand it or not." ~ Bob Proctor

The action word is:

Responsibility. Accountability, the authority to act and take decisions independently. Responsibility involves your response to something or someone. Your main responsibility is to you. Are you going to simply sit back and allow situations to dictate you? Or are you going to take responsible action? Do you actually need to respond to every situation? What response would help you, what would make you feel good? Deal with your life head on.

"The power of intuitive understanding will protect you from harm until the end of your days" ~ Lao Tsu
"The words from within are your greatest guide" ~ Sophia Johnson

CHAPTER FOUR

Being aware of signs

I was trying to 'find me.' I knew I was ready to go back home by now. My kids needed stability and normality. I was able to work hard and buy my home and a new car while working. This was a turning point for me, as I felt secure yet mobile, and able to feed my family. I was still alone though in the sense that my family and friends never really asked me how I was feeling. They simply presumed that as I was managing, I was feeling alright; but in truth I was searching for love and companionship to lighten my load. I had made friends with work colleagues and we would meet socially, which was nice. They were a more relaxed bunch than I was used to. I made friends with a guy who had much in common with me: he had two children, he was an active parent, he had recently had a breakup, his parents were a similar age as mine and we worked in the same place, he too was searching for a companion, he too was working to make a difference. And yes, we started to date, (after a considerable amount of time). He would come over with his sons, and our children would all play together and we would talk and laugh about work. After a year of dating we decided to move in together and to a bigger home. This was difficult decision for me. He also worked hard, and I wanted to support him. These were the reasons why I stuck with him. When we argued, it was about things and others outside of the relationship, things that other people had commented on. These arguments happened weekly but I persevered through them. We married a few years later; it was like a celebrity wedding. But although I had perhaps found the right man, I also, perhaps, had not yet dealt with the issue of *me*!

Message: face your fears

Working on yourself doesn't imply that you have major issues or problems. It may just mean that you wish to not just live, but live your life to the fullest. You have to know what you really want, be happy and be able to share your personal qualities with others. When you avoid living your life to the fullest you risk coming up against the same old brick wall, because the life experiences that you can learn from are always addressed from the same old angle. Face your fears head on, come out of your comfort zone, try to approach things differently; and the results can be amazing!

The action word is:

Awareness. This gives you clarification of the direction in which you are going, and enables you to understand yourself. We have all felt a certain sense of anxiety from time to time, as though a voice from within is saying 'don't go there' or 'are you sure?' If you open your eyes, listen to your heart, be aware of your feelings, and focus on how you feel, the signs are clear to see, like traffic signals displaying what is right. Iylana Vanzant's book *Faith in the Valley* speaks about being confined to a metaphorical valley until you realise the lesson which is to be learnt from your present experience, at which point you can escape the valley. Have awareness in all circumstances. Be fully present in each moment.

"Happiness is not something you postpone for the future, it is something you design for the present" ~ Brian Mayne
"Joy attracts joy" ~ Sophia Johnson

CHAPTER FIVE

Appreciating your growth

Self love

When I was still teaching young adults, studying and working for myself, I began attending motivational lectures. Many things jumped out at me. One question in particular touched home: how would your child/children describe you? The thought cut like a knife: I had strength, resilience, courage: many attributes, but I wasn't using them in the right way. I also read a book which made me realise that I was blocking my own dreams and aspirations, and surrounding myself with the wrong people. But I had a choice, too.

I have always had a close relationship with my grandfather. I helped him as he grew older, and he relied on me to sort out his business. I took him to a solicitor's appointment one day, and as I sat there with him I broke down in tears. I then started to ask myself why I was crying. I had a paradigm shift, and everything was so clear. When I returned home that evening I sat my husband down and expressed to him my fear that if I was to die tomorrow, my children would feel empty and alone. He replied that that was my business.

You may know by now that my grandmother was my hero; she was always giving, and full of love. But she was also always so unhappy with herself, and just wanted someone to love her. She was an orphan, so she loved her kids, and her husband too; but he didn't give back as much as she gave out, and she died at just 56, waiting for things to happen, not *making* her life happen. I saw, on my day of emotional realisation, that I was heading the same way as my Nan.

Message: no going back

Imagine a funfair ride which you don't want to go on, but do anyway in order to join in with your friends. As you sit on the ride, your stomach is in knots and you want to escape, but don't want anyone to notice your anxiety. The fairground music begins to play and the ride creaks into motion. There is no going back now. It's a new experience which seems daunting yet exciting. Understand that you can be influenced by others, but that really it is better to make decisions yourself and feel energised by the challenge posed, because you made the choice. In my experience, I reached a breaking point; I was silently screaming for the inner me to be unleashed.

The action word is:

Focus. You need to keep your focus on your goals; this is when you need to find tools, skills, and people who inspire you. Tools could be inspirational self-help books just like this one; or goal maps, planning what you wish to achieve and why, what, how and when. Skills are appropriate actions you will undertake to achieve focus. People are a key function of your focus, as generally when you are focused some people will not understand or will not provide support. Focus involves your self-awareness of what you are going to do, and the courage to keep your eye on the goal no matter what obstacles might appear. It is essential to plan some 'focus time' into your life, and stick to it: each step takes you a little closer to what you want. Love yourself enough to keep focusing on your goals and committing yourself to achieving them.

"You are never too old to set another goal or to dream a new dream" ~ C.S. Lewis
"Create a better life" ~ Sophia Johnson

CHAPTER SIX

Understanding that a renewal is necessary

New beginnings

Each experience, each obstacle, is a life lesson. From the chapters in this book, with the awareness and knowledge and wisdom I have now, I can clearly see the direction, the path I was supposed to take. I have had many experiences to which I was blind, where I was not connecting with the real me; and I can see now the opportunity that was in front of me at the time. Does this upset me? No, not at all. This is what has made me the woman and mother I am today; I have no regrets, and I give thanks for these experiences, as they have strengthened me. I always knew that I was here for a purpose; I knew that I was going to be ok, I had an inner flame. Some of the maxims that ring truest for me personally are "lean not on your own understanding", give all your burdens to the Lord,' and 'take power in prayer.' Ask yourself whether ignoring a problem will merely allow it to manifest, or build up, or reoccur even more strongly. When I decided to give my burdens to the Lord it made me realise that I was giving them away for a greater good, to someone who is able to resolve them, so that I had no further reason to worry. This isn't to say that you will find comfort in the same way, but I feel a duty to help you understand that I have found my peace and I am happy with my new life, hence the reason I have written this book. As a speaker once said in a sermon, failure is a noun and not a verb, an event not a person, an action not a lifetime. So—*move on* from failure.

Message:

There comes a time in all of our lives when we have just had enough, and deep down we know that we have to make changes. That may be why you are reading this book, because you are searching for motivation, or inspirational words to strengthen you.

The action word is:

Purpose. The reason for which something exists, or for which it has been done or made. Make a list of things you enjoy, that you are good at. Ask yourself the following questions:

What am I grateful for?

. . . .
. . . .
. . . .
. . . .

What are my talents?

. . . .
. . . .
. . . .
. . . .

What are my skills?

. . . .
. . . .
. . . .
. . . .

What will I enjoy doing for the rest of my life?

. . . .
. . . .
. . . .
. . . .

What can I do each day to ensure I am happy?

. . . .
. . . .
. . . .
. . . .

What can I give back?

. . . .
. . . .
. . . .
. . . .

CHAPTER SEVEN

Making it happen and moving forward

My journey

In devising a plan to work to, I wrote my goals and pictured how I saw them. Then, each goal had to be broken down into a timeline: when I was going to start on the goal, and when it was to be achieved by. My goals were then broken down further, looking at what I had to do to achieve them, where I need to be, what skills I need to have. Getting rid of negativity, and possibly distancing yourself from negative people, can be the hard part there; but it is important. Personally I had to list the people who I felt were draining me of energy, and tell myself that if those people should call, it was *my* time, and I could not speak or could only converse for a limited time. My tools were my goal map, quotes, and time set aside for devotion to God. An acronym I like for being a great role model is to be always pressing PLAY: Positively Living, Action, YOU. All these elements, used often, and with a degree of planning, create the recipe for successful, positive pursuit of desires, and hopefully you can gain new skills, friends, and knowledge along the way.

Message:

Love your new beginnings, as your journey is just that, a new start. You may have to work for it, but you may also develop a profound appreciation and gratitude for your journey.

The action word is:

Embrace. Embrace your experiences and your transformation; enjoy them. Obstacles occur in life but they can bring you strength. Love your life and be grateful for all things. Think 'I am here'—you are here because there is a plan, and a journey, for you to seize; so make it a joyful one.

What follows is a template, which I have used myself, to support you in planning your journey and actions. By answering the questions it poses, you are in essence giving yourself a personal audit. The formula hopefully allows you to see what you are really doing and where you are heading.

The goal process—planning your success:

Goal/Dream (what do I want?)
Order (what are my priorities, in achieving goals?)
Draw/Imagine (what does each goal or dream look like?)
Why (why do I want to achieve my goals?)
When/Timeline (when do I want to achieve my goals?)
How (how will I achieve my goals)? Training or new skills
    may be involved)
Who/Organisations (whose help will I need, in achieving
    my goals?)

Reason WHY:

Main GOAL:

'Sub' Goals:

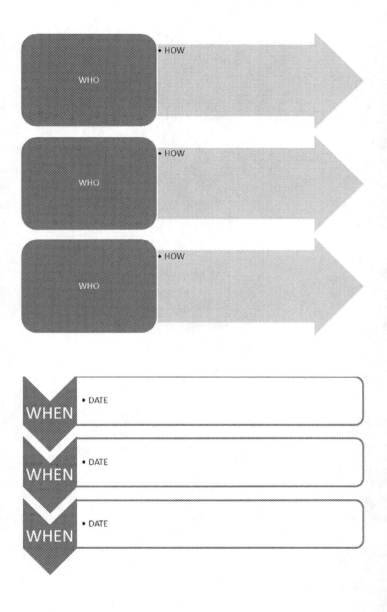

Date:
Signature:

Having a clear plan gives you direction, and points of action to implement daily. You can add to the plan when you have accomplished a task, or when you begin to build your confidence. Your goals will be easier to digest if a clear plan or template to implement them is formed, like a picture in your mind. Then, even subconsciously perhaps, you can constantly be working on or thinking about achievable actions that, in keeping with the plan you've formulated, will further your goals.

"Follow your honest convictions and stay strong" ~ William
Thackeray
"We must inspire ourselves by believing we have the power to
accomplish everything we set out to do" ~ Iyanla Vanzant
"Change is inevitable; growth is optional" ~ Unknown

CHAPTER EIGHT

Giving your life power

Your attitude and mind set are key to making what
changes are necessary to be successful and to develop as a
person, especially if, like I have, you face many daunting
hurdles along the way. Replace negative thoughts with
positive ones wherever you can. I often give people a common
tip: limit your 'pity party' to two minutes at the most. Also,
when something troublesome comes up, ask yourself three
questions: 1) What would happen if I leave this issue to
manifest? 2) How does this situation aid me? 3) Why
would I not deal with this now? Once you have answered
these questions truthfully, you may see that the issue is not
worth bothering with at all. Or, maybe, it can be dealt with
straight away, after which you can move on. Or, perhaps you
will find yourself able to simply rebuke the negative thoughts
or issues which are threatening to take hold of you. As you
start to focus on you and what you are going to accomplish,
things happen; people from your past may even appear. I,
for example, was pestered by one guy who always seemed to
call me when I was going through any kind of relationship

turmoil. It was as if he contacted me as some sort of test. In the early days of this, I would talk to him on the phone, thinking I was being pleasant. When, though, during my transitional stage of change, he predictably asked me out, I thought "oh please" and I just had to politely say that I would call him, and he shouldn't call me. I cut the call off and threw the phone on the bed, shouting out loud "I rebuke that." It was not that I was telling him off as such, but I was abruptly rejecting the negativity in me that he was building up. And I haven't received another call from him. It may seem funny, but it works: create what you want in your life, spurn anything or anyone you don't want; speak out when you are alone, bring forth and attract goodness into your life. And life's challenges are easier to tackle once you have contemplated them and thought about your options.

These days, I have been through a lot. I have only talked about my drama as a reflective way of giving readers something to empathise with and relate to. But I have no regrets, merely experiences which I have learnt from, and which make me the woman I am today. I have gained the strength and faith to always pull through, and a heightened determination to feel joy, happiness and love. My life is filled with things I like and with people whose company I enjoy, and my mind is always thinking positive thoughts. I am present in every moment; meaning that each moment has a role to play in advancing me forward in the right direction. Some more questions I ask myself, and you can ask yourself too, are as follows:

1. What am I getting from what I am doing? (when watching TV, for example)

. . . .
. . . .

2. When I am speaking, am I attracting good or bad in my life?

. . . .

. . . .

3. What have I done today to make me laugh?

. . . .

. . . .

4. Have I given support to anybody today?

. . . .

. . . .

5. What am I willing to do?

. . . .

. . . .

6. What am I willing to give up?

. . . .

. . . .

7. Do I have the right network of people around me?

. . . .

. . . .

8. Have I stepped out of my comfort zone today?

. . . .

. . . .

9. Are the actions that I am taking fulfilling my purpose?

. . . .

. . . .

10. Am I willing to embrace new concepts?

. . . .

. . . .

11. Have I rested today?

. . . .

. . . .

Success is measured by how *you* feel, by *your* peace of mind. It is not defined in relation to other people's successes, whether real or perceived. It will be characterised by where you have been, whaw you have experienced, how you have mastered situations, how you have developed. Give your life power by confidently being accountable for your actions, and taking control. You may reach a moment in your life when you begin to think 'what makes me happy?' Be grateful every day for the things you have, for what you have accomplished, for your health, for your children, for your life, for the fact that your life is continuing to unfold. This mind set, of thankfulness, will attract yet more things to you, to be thankful for. Ask yourself 'What do I really signify?' 'What do I want to signify?' 'How can I change me for the better?' This is the time to reflect on your successes, and enjoy every aspect of it; to list the challenges you have overcome even when all seemed hopeless . . . in fact, why not start the reflecting right here and now?!

"Reputation is for a period of time, character is for eternity" ~
J.B. Gough
"Difficulties mastered are opportunities won" ~ Winston
Churchill

FINAL MESSAGE

Your story is not about anyone else, it comes from within. Push through and create the life you wish to live, go after what you want, let go of anything that, or anyone who, makes you feel undeserving and judged. Trying to please everyone won't work; you need to please yourself first. This doesn't mean being selfish, but rather acting in a way which 'gets the most out of you', and will allow you to be of greatest benefit to the people around you. If you show leadership, step by step, day by day, week by week, month by month you will get stronger and more focused, and each vision and dream you have will begin to manifest into reality. A future cannot be based on the past, but can be built on top of it; if you recognise the lessons you have learned and design a path to take you forward. Be truthful to yourself, and practise the habit of visualising, planning and taking action.

Life still goes on around you. Challenges still present themselves, but when your mind is occupied with building a better you, with self-development, external issues no longer control you. Your thoughts benefits you, instead of burdening you. Identify only with things which uplift and motivate you, not with things that conspire to bring you down.

Many people talk about what they want to do, or what others are doing that they find inspirational. These people often tend to be the ones who continue to speak year after year, yet never take action, or give up at the first obstacle. Believe me when I say: keep going, keep planning; one door will open another for you, as you become ever more equipped to apply yourself in different ways to life's challenges, and as you more deeply understand that your life and your story are vessels for your individual achievements. We each have great triumphs to accomplish. Your destiny may not be as a Michelin star chef, but you could use your culinary skills to feed communities in need, for example. Your calling might not be to become a famous actor or actress, but perhaps you own an art and drama studio, and your skills are needed in that capacity. These are examples. All you have to really remember is that you are here for a purpose, and that you have to fulfil that destiny to the fullest in order to be as happy, and as deservingly happy, as you can be.

Until you start, you will never know. The things you may tell yourself, the excuses that you make in order to put off beginning a new journey, may be just that—excuses. And meanwhile, people around you may be getting on with changing their lives, and doing what they need to do for a better life, while you are left somewhat floundering, stuck in a rut, repeating the 'ifs', the 'buts' and the 'maybes'. Don't let your story end up being 'if only'. You deserve better than that.

I sat down one day, alone, simply meditating. I thought about what I was doing, about my family, about what makes me happy. Given the great relationship I have with my grandfather, I reminisced on our past conversations. What stood out to me was the importance of time; how it moves on even if we are standing still, and the degree to which we are ageing each day as time marches swiftly forward. I want to be able to look back and feel, always in the forefront of my mind, good feelings which encompass my appreciation of life. The process of looking back and being able to pick out the good from it is something like having a childhood scar: at the time it was painful and by no means funny, but that pain is no longer there, and you may even joke about it now. So, try not to keep taking yourself back to the pain, the negativity of the past; that won't be of benefit to you. Instead, move on, mindful of what you have learned, and confident in your awareness that bad experiences were then, but not now. Some people, unfortunately, are not able to embrace change, and are in a sense locked in to the past. There may be many reasons for this, poverty and cultural expectations being two examples. Such people struggle in many ways but they also have many things which they can be grateful for and can make a success of. You always have the choice to take control and 'seize the day', creating your new beginning and new life. To realise this, you need the courage and persistence to keep on going, no matter what. Different transitional stages take their course in our lives, like the changing of the seasons or the tides of the sea, but keep an unwavering ownership of the choices that you make, and ask how each phase, each decision, aids you.

I am happy, every day, to apply myself, to be bold in my walk, and to seek contentment. I have mentioned my faith in God; and I am given to believe that God wants me to fulfil my life's purpose. Through my faith, I share my memoirs to support people, to motivate others to give thanks for their situation, and to do the right thing in positively changing lives. I will end with a passage from the New International Version of the Bible, namely Matthew: 7: 7-12. "Ask and it will be given to you; seek and you will find; knock and the door will be opened to you. For everyone who asks receives; the one who seeks finds; and to the one who knocks, the door will be opened. Which of you, if your son asks for bread, will give him a stone? Or if he asks for a fish, will give him a snake? If you, then, though you are evil, know how to give good gifts to your children, how much more will your Father in heaven give good gifts to those who ask him! So in everything, do to others what you would have them do to you, for this sums up the Law and the Prophets." So, treat others as you wish to be treated, go after the desires of your heart, and I trust that the words I have written in this book will help to support you on your journey. I believe in your success.

"It is not length of life, but depth of life." ~ Ralph Waldo Emerson

FURTHER READING

How to Get Out Of Your Own Way ~ Tyrese Gibson
Goal Mapping ~ Brian Mayne
Power Thoughts ~ Joyce Meyer
The Secret ~ Rhonda Byrne
Super Rich ~ Russell Simmons
The Power ~ Rhonda Byrne
Faith in the Valley ~ Iyanla Vanzant
Aspire ~ Kevin Hall
The Holy Bible (NIV version)

About the Author

Sophia Johnson M.A.S.C (Lifecoach), businesswoman, and mother, like each of us, has been on her own journey of self-discovery, using her personal experiences and turning it around positively, facilitating workshops furthermore encouraging through speaker events that empower individuals to embrace change as well as challenges establishing a better life.

If you would like to have more information go to:
www.diamondvisioncic.co.uk
www.diamondvisioncic.com
or email: *sophia@diamondvisioncic.co.uk*

Printed in the United States
By Bookmasters